THE DNA OF GUTSY LEADERS

Study Guide

Terence H. Biggs II & Dr. Sharon M. Biggs

ISBN 978-1-53008-139-4

PREFACE

This study guide is a comprehensive tool for use during and after studying the practical leadership principles outlined in the book, *The DNA of Gutsy Leaders: I'm Made for This Moment!* After you have completed your course of study, use this guide often and use it well to apply the attainable gutsy leadership principles to your own experiences.

Develop your own gutsy style of leadership by applying the practical ideas embedded in the book's narratives.

Navigate the road map provided by the book's featured 21st century gutsy leaders to help you construct the leadership journey you are wired for.

Accept your personal leadership wiring and seize the moments you're made for!

Table of Contents

Overview   1

Syllabus   2

Session One   4

Session Two   5

Session Three   8

Session Four   10

Session Five   13

Session Six   14

Session Seven   15

Session Eight   17

Session Nine   18

Session Ten   19

About the Authors   20

Contact Information   21

INTRODUCTION

What's the big deal about gutsy leadership?

Leaders exist in every culture, phase and walk of life. Some people lead in their homes while others lead in environments outside of the home. Whatever the venue, frontline leadership requires that individuals regularly take actions designed to benefit the people and groups that look to the leaders for direction.

Because situations evolve when life happens as we're leading other human beings, leaders are called to be bold and courageous enough to know what to do, when to do it, and who to do it for. *It takes guts* to lead in such a fluid and ambiguous way since the people following a leader might not always understand exactly how the leader is leading, and why he or she is or is not taking certain actions.

How to use this study guide

Each of the 10 sections of this tool will help guide the study of leadership narrative chapters from our book, *The DNA of Gutsy Leaders: I'm Made for This Moment!* Course participants are encouraged to read each chapter of the book before taking the course and highlight sections and pages that resonate with leadership experiences they've either had or observed in others in the past.

Reading book chapters ahead of time will assist participants so they can actively engage in activities and conversations that surface during the **10 one-hour sessions**.

Through deep study and analysis of the leadership narratives, course participants will be guided to first, identify and second, embrace their own gutsy leadership attributes and styles. Once this happens, people who might not have regarded themselves as gutsy leaders because of past preconceived notions about what gutsy leadership can look like, will be better positioned and better informed to embrace and respond to their individual big and small leadership moments.

Enjoy the leadership course and the discussions that stem from it as you embrace the gutsy leadership moments you were made for!

Terence H. Biggs II and Dr. Sharon M. Biggs, Co-Authors
The DNA of Gutsy Leaders: I'm Made for This Moment! ©2015

STUDY GUIDE OVERVIEW

The purpose of this study guide is to provide a leadership development road map from 21st century gutsy leaders wired to lead people and organizations through change.

Course participants will engage in leadership conversations about topics generated by the book, THE DNA OF GUTSY LEADERS by Biggs & Biggs (2015). The authenticity woven throughout the discussion prompts will help current and aspiring leaders identify, develop and hone their personal gutsy leadership skills sets and acumen.

Everyone is encouraged to journal personal takeaways from the course and use the takeaways to help develop his or her personal leadership mission statements and action plans for implementation.

Course Prerequisite:
Read the book: The DNA of Gutsy Leaders (Biggs & Biggs, 2015)

Course Title: *The DNA of Gutsy Leaders*
Course Subtitle: I'm Made For This Moment!

Course Description

The DNA of Gutsy Leaders: I'm Made For This Moment! is designed to deepen each student's understanding of how to identify and embrace gutsy leadership principles while seizing all of the leadership moments he/she was made for.

Course Objectives

Students will gain deeper knowledge and understanding of the following:

- The Meaning of Gutsy Leadership
- Profiling Individual Gutsy Leadership
- The Power of Self-Reflection for Gutsy Leaders
- Common Trends Among Successful 21st Century Gutsy Leaders
- The Role of Intuition and Courage
- Finding Your Gutsy Leadership Brand
- Gutsy Evolution & the Clarion Call
- DNA Wiring
- Gutsy Marketplace Leadership
- Capitalizing On Our Marketplace Moments
- Identifying Leadership Moments We Are Made For
- Thriving in Our Leadership Moments

Course Requirements:

Attendance – The course runs 10 sessions. Students are required to attend all 10 sessions. If an emergency develops, please notify the instructors.

Participation – Participation during class discussions is encouraged, anticipated and appreciated.

Reading Assignments – Students are expected to read all reading assignments prior to class and then be prepared to add their voices to classroom discussions.

Written Assignments – Students are expected to complete written assignments prior to class. Completed written assignments will be used during group discussions and will be collected and reviewed at the instructors' discretion.

Evaluation – At the conclusion of the semester, you will be given a class evaluation. Please complete the evaluation thoroughly and thoughtfully and submit it before you leave the classroom. The evaluation will help us know how to improve future course offerings.

Required Text:

Biggs, Dr. Sharon M. and Terence H. <u>The DNA of Gutsy Leaders</u>
Subtitle: I'm Made For This Moment!

Lesson: Introduction | DNA Moments | Clarion Call

Pre-Assignment: THE DNA OF GUTSY LEADERS – Read Pages 9-10 and 175-178

ACTIVITY #1 Prompt –
- Work with a partner to flowchart 5 things you've learned about each of the authors' leadership journeys. Think about one area that resonated with your personal leadership journey and be prepared to share out with the whole group.
- The instructor(s) will extract highlights from the chapters and invite Q&A from the group.

20 minutes including whole-group Q&A

DNA Moments (Pages 9 – 10)
ACTIVITY #2 Prompt –
How did one of the bulleted items on pages 9-10 present a challenge to your personal leadership? Talk in groups of 2 to 3 about that experience and about what you *would now do differently* at this phase of your leadership journey based on what you now know about leadership.

15 minutes *including small-group conversations*

Clarion Call For Gutsy Leaders (Pg175 – 178)
ACTIVITY #3 Prompt –
Watch the leadership video clip – "Remember the Titans"
https://www.youtube.com/watch?v=0VZW54uJW4s

Instructor(s) will discuss 3 main points of emphasis that correspond with the message of the video clip – *a)* Used to having people vacillate between loving and hating them *b)* Are tradition shifters when necessary *c)* Get results

20 minutes *including discussion and 2 minutes, 41 seconds for video*

Session One Closure (5 minutes)

Home Learning Activity for Session 2 – Reread pages 13 - 42 (Dr. James Caulfield).

Lesson: Gutsy Leadership Defined

The Meaning of Gutsy Leadership - Dr. James Caulfield (Pages 13 – 42)

ACTIVITY #1 Prompt –
Take some minutes to reflect on and assess your own leadership by scoring yourself on the "Awareness of Gutsy Leadership Profile" in this section. Once you've scored yourself, score Dr. Caulfield based on what you've read about him on pages 13 to 42. Talk briefly with a partner about similarities and differences in how you scored yourself and how you scored Dr. Caulfield. Remember to talk about the "why" during your conversation.
25 minutes including partner turn-and-talk

Score Yourself on Awareness of Gutsy Leadership Profile

Think about your leadership over the past three (3) years:

Never (1)   Rarely (2)   Sometimes   (3) Often   (4)   Almost always (5)

1.   I tell people what's on my mind even when the messages are difficult ones to deliver and to hear.   **1 2 3 4 5**

2.   When I know someone has been let down by me (whether I've done something wrong or not) I quickly and willingly do things to regain their confidence in my leadership.
                                                     1 2 3 4 5

3.   I lead based on my belief system and personal convictions about issues even when my actions are not popular.   **1 2 3 4 5**

4.   I look for people who are more skilled and expert in certain areas than I am who can be part of my team.   **1 2 3 4 5**

5.   I am mission-driven and find that there are times when not everyone is on the same mission bus I'm driving.   **1 2 3 4 5**

6.   I say yes to right fits and say no to wrong fits.   **1 2 3 4 5**

7. Just when I think I'm being a talking head someone I'm leading will articulate something I've said or carry out an action based on what I've said needs to happen.

1 2 3 4 5

8. I lead by navigating the political tides of a system.

1 2 3 4 5

9. I am authentic and consistent in my leadership.

1 2 3 4 5

10. I want to always be right when I make leadership decisions and I insist that others see me as being right.

1 2 3 4 5

Total Score

Overall score of 25 or less = it's time to pay attention to your leadership style.

Overall score of 26–43 = healthy range of gutsy leadership but needing some focus on your leadership style.

Overall score of 44 or above = **Congratulations**, you are flowing in your gutsy leadership style and building your personal and team capacity!

ACTIVITY # 2 Prompt –

"The Last Word" activity. In groups of 4 or 5 one person cites and reads aloud a sentence or paragraph from pages 13 to 42 that reflects one of the bulleted concepts below. **After reading the passage aloud the person says nothing else.** Each member of the group takes a turn responding to the reading passage, starting with the person to the right of the reader, etc. *Only one person can speak at a time*. After each person has responded to the reading passage select a group member to write your group's takeaways on one of the large chart papers and to use **3 minutes** to share the big ideas with the large group.

25 minutes including big idea sharing and charting of ideas

Dr. James Caulfield's Chapter – pages 13 – 42 – Activity #2 prompts
o Speak What's On Your Mind
o Be Proactive
o Lead From Your Core & Be a Bold Pioneer
o Assess Whose Needs You Are Meeting
o Your DNA Guides You To The Right Position For You
o Take Action When People Get Disappointed in You
o Surround Yourself with Ambitious Folks to Help Seize Your Leadership Moments
o People Listen Even When They Dislike You
o Try to Learn the Network's Political Fabric and Culture
o Choose Battles Wisely & Always Act on the Basis of Sound Principle and Virtue
o Let Integrity Win…Your Opposition…Find the Table…Sit Down…Join the Feast

Session 2 Closure (10 minutes)

Home Learning Activity for Session 3 –
Re-read pages 13 – 42 (Dr. James Caulfield). Think about a leadership situation of yours that failed. How and why did it fail?

Lesson: Chapter about Dr. James Caulfield (pages 13-42)

ACTIVITY # 1 Prompt –
Watch leadership video clip – "I Love Lucy, The Chocolate Factory"
https://www.youtube.com/watch?v=kRC3BiOig6w

ACTIVITY # 2 Prompt –
Fishbone Activity – Using a fishbone chart, work with 2 to 3 people to map out what was attempted and what failed in the video.

Then, use a separate fishbone chart to map out one of your personal failed leadership attempts and the factors that might have contributed to the failure. Discuss with a partner the *personal failure* you fishboned about and then share an outsider's perspective about what might have caused your partner's failure.

20 minutes including partner discussion

ACTIVITY # 3 Prompt –
Personal Reflection Activity – Describe your own gutsy leadership journey based on the following prompts. Be sure to include any relevant failed attempts.

15 minutes including sharing with the whole group by one or two people

Describe an experience when you attempted to be an inclusive leader when building a team. Why did it succeed or fail?

****

When have you tried to lead from the front? What was the outcome?

****

What have you done when members of your team have opposed each other? What worked?
What didn't work?
****

What gutsy leadership legacy do you believe you'll most be remembered for?
****

ACTIVITY # 4 Prompt –
Watch leadership video clip – "The Lion King – Scar & Mufasa"
https://www.youtube.com/watch?v=-8wgXRNYcPM

ACTIVITY #5 – Talk with table partners about Mufasa's leadership based on the short
video clip. Refer to leadership strategies discussed throughout pages 13-42 to highlight how
Mufasa led beyond power trips to exemplify gutsy leadership.

5 minutes

a) Be an Inclusive Leader & Strategically Plan & Help People Remember Your Legacy
b) See Growth & Excitement Potential in Every Challenge & Add the Right People to Your Team
c) Be Visible and Relational & Lead From the Front
d) Stop the Infighting Before it Stunts Your Vision
e) Build a Legacy That's Tough to Follow
f) Create Organizations and Systems Fit for Dignitaries
g) Lead Beyond Failures and Power Trips
h) Play the Game - Win Some, Lose Some
i) You Control The Agenda
j) Transform an Organization One System at a Time
k) Try New Things With Pilot Initiatives to Help People Move Beyond Their Fears
l) Gutsy DNA Legacy & Have The Guts to Withstand Coercive Persuasion

Session 3 Closure (5 minutes)

Home Learning Activity for Session 4 –
Read pages 43 – 65 (Judy & Jack Killion). Think about a leadership situation you had to
restart once it got off the ground. How did you view the re-start? How did others view it?
What was the outcome?

9

SESSION FOUR

Lesson: Chapters about Judy & Jack Killion (pages 43-65)

ACTIVITY # 1 Prompt –
One participant reads aloud "A Mindset to Succeed" on page 50 of the book.

As a large group discuss how Judy Chapman used a success mindset to restart and overcome leadership challenges and relate the discussion points to your own leadership experiences that had to be restarted.

10 minutes including group discussion

ACTIVITY # 2 Prompt –
The instructor(s) will extract highlights from pages 43-65 and invite Q&A from the whole group.

20 minutes including Q&A

Finding Opportunities in Chaos – Judy Chapman Killion (Pages 43 – 51)
- o Identify and Seize Your Moments
- o A Mindset to Succeed
- o Be True To Your Own Definition
- o Press Restart if you Need To

Be Willing To Do Things – Jack Killion (Pages 53 – 65)
- o Be Ready to Experience Different Leadership Moments
- o Be Clear About What You Want and Don't Want
- o Trying Something New Takes Guts
- o Shift Gears To Seize Opportunities
- o There Will Be Challenges Even When There's Success
- o Search For Who Wants Your Coaching
- o Be a Thinker and Take Chances
- o Assemble a Coaching and Advisory Team

ACTIVITY # 3 Prompt –

Engage in 1-minute partner speed conversations about different topics from pages 43-65 that will be provided by the group facilitators. Relate the topics to your personal leadership experiences. <u>Be ready to switch partners and topics when you hear the signal from the facilitators</u>.

10 minutes including partner and topic switches

ACTIVITY # 4 Prompt –

Watch leadership video clip of "Black Hawk Down"
https://www.youtube.com/watch?v=AUJ6cxWdZwA

Instructor(s) will lead a conversation about leadership characteristics from pages 9 to 10 of the book demonstrated in the video clip.

10 minutes for conversation

Gutsy Leadership Characteristics from pages 9 to 10:

Gutsy leaders see and hear where bullets are shot from but they don't sweat or flinch – they continue leading forward to squash the enemy.

Gutsy leaders view the enemy as nothing more than a deliberate distraction designed to destroy purpose and mission.

Gutsy leaders can become apologetic when asking for help as if asking for help is a display of weakness versus a demonstration of wisdom.

Gutsy leaders instinctively take a strategically defensive stance when attacks are hurled at them.

Gutsy leaders remain clinical yet compassionate in order to keep emotions in check.

Gutsy leaders take severe and personal hits at very close range.

Gutsy leaders engage in intense fights that might take all day or all night because they're determined to reach the problem, wrap their minds and arms around the problem, and then lead others to solve the problem.

Gutsy leaders refuse to leave any wounded behind to die without first trying to rescue them even when the wounded don't know they need rescuing.

Gutsy leaders can be easily misread by people who misinterpret their clinical compassion as being non-relational detachment and disconnectedness.

Gutsy leaders stay above deadly political minutiae and keep their ears to the ground so they clearly hear and respond to rumblings.

Gutsy leaders get thrust into impossible situations and they are wired to produce successful outcomes.

Gutsy leaders are brave enough to either be on the front line or strategically position others to be on the front line to win battles and conquer the enemy.

Gutsy leaders are not excuse makers. They dive in, strategize and confront problems.

Session 4 Closure (5 minutes)

Home Learning Activity for Session 5 –
Read pages 67 – 80 (Rev. Dr. Dharius Daniels). Think about how purpose, trust and strategy impact leadership practices.

Lesson: Chapter about Rev. Dr. Dharius Daniels (pages 67-80)

ACTIVITY # 1 Prompt –

Instructors extract highlights from pages 67-80. Invite Q&A from the whole group.

50 minutes including Q&A

Intuitive and Courageous – Dr. Dharius Daniels (Pages 67 – 80)

- Be Clear About Your Purpose
- Have The Self-Confidence To Go Up Against Giants
- Be Strong, Courageous and Decisive
- Guard The Trust of Others
- Avoid Moving at the Speed of Profit and be Authentic
- Essential Things Might Not Be Easy Things To Achieve
- Assess What People Need and Coach Them on Those Areas
- Embrace Your Personal Wiring
- Strategic Leadership
- Creativity Still Needs Timeliness

Session 5 Closure (10 minutes)

Home Learning Activity for Session 6 –

Read pages 81 – 92 (Rev. Dr. Dharius Daniels).

SESSION SIX

Lesson: Chapter about Rev. Dr. Dharius Daniels (pages 81-92)

ACTIVITY # 1 Prompt –
Instructors extract highlights from pages 81-92. Invite Q&A from the whole group.

50 minutes including Q&A

- Culture of Incessant Tinkering
- No Room For Mediocrity
- Cast The Vision so There's Buy-In
- Focus on Authenticity
- Start With Perspective
- Know What You Do Well
- Create a Culture of Transparent Discourse
- The Value of Experience
- Guts to be Radically Different
- Emphasize the DNA of Gutsy Leadership

Session 6 Closure (10 minutes)

Home Learning Activity for Session 7 –
Read pages 93 – 111 (Mr. Peter Grandich & Mr. Anthony Beshara).

SESSION SEVEN

Lesson: Chapters about Peter Grandich & Anthony Beshara (pages 93-111)

ACTIVITY # 1 Prompt –
Watch decision making video clip of "The Big Bang Theory" (*Going to the Movies*)
https://www.youtube.com/watch?v=SPZRtlqBgYk

ACTIVITY # 2 Prompt –
With a partner discuss how any leadership strategies on pages 93-111 were depicted in the video clip.

As a whole group discuss how fear sometimes impedes a leader's ability to make a sound decision. The instructor(s) will lead a talk based on pages 93-111 about how leaders can overcome fear when they are attempting to make decisions.

35 minutes including partner and whole-group talk

Willing To Take The Lumps – Peter Grandich (Pages 93 – 104)
- Make Sound Decisions
- Fear Can Be A Reaction for Leaders
- Keep Your Leadership Game Face On
- Lead With Compassion and Humility
- Identify What You Need To Personally Improve

Different Messages Motivate Leaders – Anthony Beshara (Pages 105 – 111)
- Be Brave Enough To Shift Traditions
- Stay Current With Trends
- Coach People To Protect The Brand
- Build Human Capital
- The Training Doesn't Stop
- Keep Everyone on One Vision Page

ACTIVITY # 3 Prompt –

On the index card you've received rate yourself on a scale from 1 to 10, with 10 being the highest, on the following:

A. Your level of professional decision making right now.
B. Your level of professional decision making where you want it to be.
C. How you believe your professional followers view your decision making.
D. Your level of personal decision making right now.
E. Your level of personal decision making where you want it to be.
F. How you believe your personal followers view your decision making.
G. The impact fear has on your decision making right now.
H. How humble and compassionate you are as a leader right now.
I. How humble and compassionate you want to be as a leader.
J. How convincing you are as a leadership coach.
K. How convincing you want to be as a leadership coach.
L. How comfortable your professional followers are with your vision.
M. How comfortable your personal followers are with your vision.

Total Score

Overall score of 60 or less = it's time to pay attention to your decision making style

Overall score of 61–99 = healthy range of decision making but needing some focus on your decision making style

Overall score of 100 or above = **Congratulations**, you are solid in your decision making style!

18 minutes including sharing out with the whole group

Session 7 Closure (5 minutes)

Home Learning Activity for Session 8 –
Read pages 113 – 134 (Mr. Victor Scudiery & Cliff and Mitzi Moore).

SESSION EIGHT

Lesson: Chapter about Cliff & Mitzi Moore and Victor Scudiery (pages 113-134)

ACTIVITY # 1 Prompt –
Mind Mapping demonstration and activity based on pages 113-134.
Individual mind mapping activity.

45 minutes including demonstrations

Go With Your Gut After Being Burned - Cliff and Mitzi Moore (Pages 113 – 122)
- o Be Specific With The Team About What You Need
- o Adjust the Plan To Keep The Purpose on Track
- o Volunteer Whenever You Can
- o Accept Your Leadership Mantle
- o Leadership Can Start During Youth So Identify Skill Sets
- o Be Open To What's Next

Take The Bull By The Horns – Victor Scudiery (Pages 123 – 134)
- o Know Your Leadership Direction Early On
- o Chart Your Own Success Despite Failed Attempts
- o The Moments Just Start Happening
- o You Might Have To Journey Without all The Details
- o Get People on The Bandwagon Even When You're Afraid
- o Lay The Foundation For People Who Will Lead After You
- o Your Foundation Gives Perspective
- o You Will Have to Fight Giants
- o Act on Ideas
- o Switch Lanes When You Need To
- o Gutsy Leading Is a Natural Thing

Session 8 Closure (5 minutes)

Home Learning Activity for Session 9 –
Read pages 137 – 151 ("It Takes Guts" and Dr. Sharon M. Biggs).

Lesson: It Takes Guts | Chapter about Dr. Sharon M. Biggs (pages 137-151)

ACTIVITY # 1 Prompt –
Instructor(s) will discuss common gutsy leadership trends and themes and extract highlights from pages 141-151 before inviting Q&A from the whole group.

50 minutes including Q&A

It Takes Guts (Pages 137 – 139)
Trends & Common Themes

It's Nothing Personal. It's Just Business – Dr. Sharon M. Biggs (Pages 141- 151)
   o Take Deep Breaths
   o Deep Messages Penetrate The Heart and Minds of Followers
   o We Stay on Track Even When We Are Tired
   o What Does It All Mean in The Moment?
   o We Do What We Believe Needs to be Done
   o Strategic Leadership Helps Overcome Challenges
   o Lead While You Find Your Brand
   o Purposeful Leadership Assignments
   o Empower Others As You Become More Empowered

Session 9 Closure (10 minutes)

Home Learning Activity for Session 10 –
Read pages 153 – 172 (Terence H. Biggs II).

SESSION TEN

Lesson: Chapter about Terence H. Biggs II (pages 153-172)

ACTIVITY # 1 Prompt –
Instructors extract highlights from pages 153-172 and invite Q&A from the whole group.

50 minutes including Q&A

Excellence Without Excuse – Terence H. Biggs II (Pages 153 – 172)
  o Stops
  o Gutsy Evolution
  o Change Adjustments – The Digital Disruption
  o Impatience
  o Disturbing The Apple Cart
  o Alone Time To Deal With Fears - Absorption Time
  o DNA Wiring
  o Execute Mode
  o Why Us?
  o Leadership Journal Entries

Session 10 Closure (10 minutes)

FINAL SESSION Home Learning Activities –
  ✓ Reread THE DNA OF GUTSY LEADERS now that you have taken this course.

  ✓ Choose one weekly strategy to focus on developing and journal about your progress. Include specifics about your successes and your failed attempts.

  ✓ Arrange to contact one other course participant at the end of each month who can serve as your Accountability Partner using the Gutsy Leadership Profile to self-assess.

  ✓ *Seize all of your personal and professional leadership moments while you still can!*

ABOUT THE AUTHORS

Terence H. Biggs II is Founder & CEO of Marketplace Dynamics, LLC, a leadership coaching, speaking and consulting agency. Terence is an entrepreneur who service marked the term, Excellence without Excuse^{SM}. Biggs is a John Maxwell Independent Certified Coach, Teacher and Speaker who is known for disturbing the proverbial apple cart because the excuse – *"it has not been done before"* – doesn't sit well with him. His guiding business principles are honesty, integrity and fairness. Biggs has hands-on experience operating, leading and consulting numerous small businesses. He's a marketing and technology geek that is well versed in communicating technical matters understandably to non-techies. Biggs' experience includes that of Entrepreneur, Author, Speaker, Marketing Executive, Financial Executive, Business Founder, Sales' Executive, Philanthropist, Product Developer, Trade Delegation Executive, Former Retail Store Owner & Operator, Non-Profit Co-Founder, Former Board Member of the Jersey Shore Convention and Visitors Bureau, Advisory Board Member of the Driven By Heroes veterans organization, and former Executive Director of a county Chamber of Commerce. His impressive business career of over thirty years spans throughout national and international borders and includes over fifteen years of experience as a Wall Street Financial Accounting Executive.

Dr. Sharon M. Biggs is an Executive Leadership Coach who for almost thirty years has filled State, District and School-Level leadership roles such as: Department of Education State Turnaround Coach, Executive Director, Leadership Coach, Assistant to the Superintendent, Principal, Assistant Principal, and Teacher Leader. Her work spans the gamut, having served in affluent, low-income, high-performing, low-performing, suburban, rural, and urban state-controlled districts. Dr. Biggs also leads the Educational Leadership Development Team at Marketplace Dynamics, LLC (MD). In addition to co-authoring *The DNA of Gutsy Leaders* with her husband and business partner, Terence H. Biggs II, she published four other books: *BIGGS-isms, Poetry Namaste, I Love You Hotter Than Hot,* and *The Silo Effect.* Her next book entitled, *Unfortunately ~ The Word No Woman Ever Wants to Hear,* a personal narrative about her cancer-free living after an early-detected breast cancer diagnosis, is scheduled to be released sometime in 2016-2017. Along with her love of writing, researching and reading, Dr. Biggs enjoys travel, sewing & crafting, fitness and spending time with family and loved ones.

EMAIL, PROFILE & WEBSITE INFORMATION:

Terence H. Biggs II
Terence.Biggs2@MarketplaceDynamics.com
https://www.linkedin.com/in/terencebiggs
http://www.MarketplaceDynamics.com

Dr. Sharon M. Biggs
DrSharonMBiggs@MarketplaceDynamics.com
http://www.linkedin.com/in/drsharonbiggs
http://www.MarketplaceDynamics.com
Publications on CreateSpace, Amazon and Barnes & Noble

Contact the authors to schedule on-site or online leadership coaching, workshops, conferences, seminars and speaking engagements.

www.ingramcontent.com/pod-product-compliance
Lightning Source LLC
Chambersburg PA
CBHW080533190526
45169CB00008B/3151